T0413669

JOSH ALLEN

SPORTS SUPERSTARS

BY REBECCA PETTIFORD

torque™

BELLWETHER MEDIA · MINNEAPOLIS, MN

TM

Torque brims with excitement
perfect for thrill-seekers of all kinds.
Discover daring survival skills, explore
uncharted worlds, and marvel at mighty
engines and extreme sports. In *Torque* books,
anything can happen. Are you ready?

This edition first published in 2024 by Bellwether Media, Inc.

No part of this publication may be reproduced in whole or in part without
written permission of the publisher. For information regarding permission,
write to Bellwether Media, Inc., Attention: Permissions Department,
6012 Blue Circle Drive, Minnetonka, MN 55343.

Library of Congress Cataloging-in-Publication Data

Names: Pettiford, Rebecca, author.
Title: Josh Allen / by Rebecca Pettiford.
Description: Minneapolis, MN : Bellwether Media, 2024. | Series: Sports
    superstars | Includes bibliographical references and index. | Audience:
    Ages 7-12 | Audience: Grades 4-6 | Summary: "Engaging images
    accompany information about Josh Allen. The combination of high-interest
    subject matter and light text is intended for students in grades 3 through
    7"– Provided by publisher.
Identifiers: LCCN 2023006477 (print) | LCCN 2023006478 (ebook) | ISBN
    9798886874648 (library binding) | ISBN 9798886876529 (ebook)
Subjects: LCSH: Allen, Josh, 1996–Juvenile literature. | Buffalo Bills
    (Football team)–Juvenile literature. | Quarterbacks
    (Football)–Biography–Juvenile literature. | Football players–United
    States–Biography–Juvenile literature.
Classification: LCC GV939.A534 P47 2024 (print) | LCC GV939.A534 (ebook)
    | DDC 796.33092 [B]–dc23/eng/20230214
LC record available at https://lccn.loc.gov/2023006477
LC ebook record available at https://lccn.loc.gov/2023006478

Editor: Rachael Barnes   Designer: Gabriel Hilger

Printed in the United States of America, North Mankato, MN.

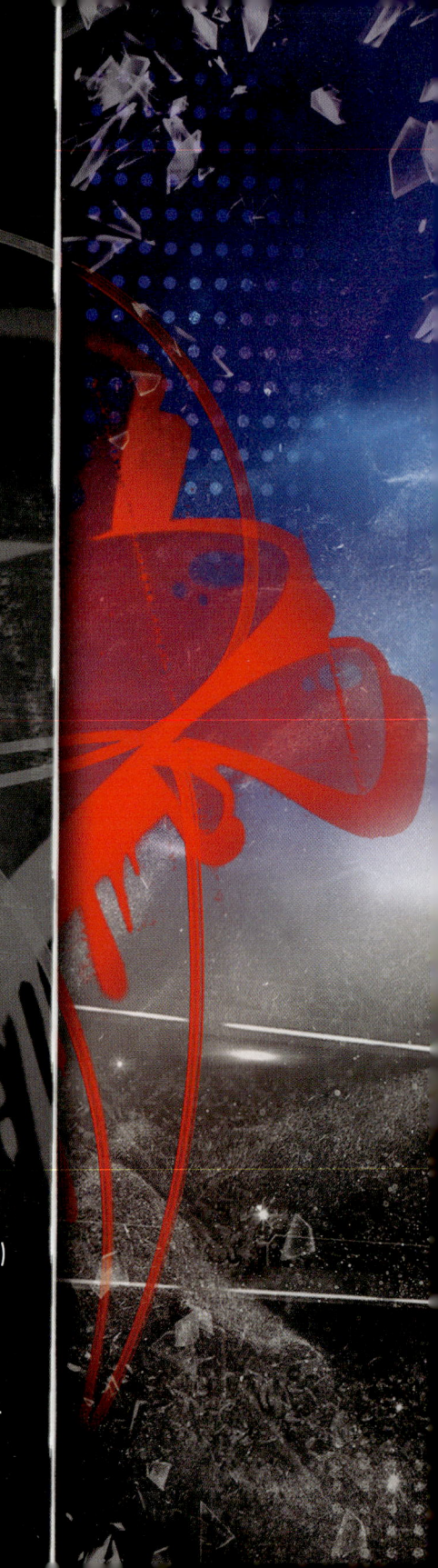

TABLE OF
CONTENTS

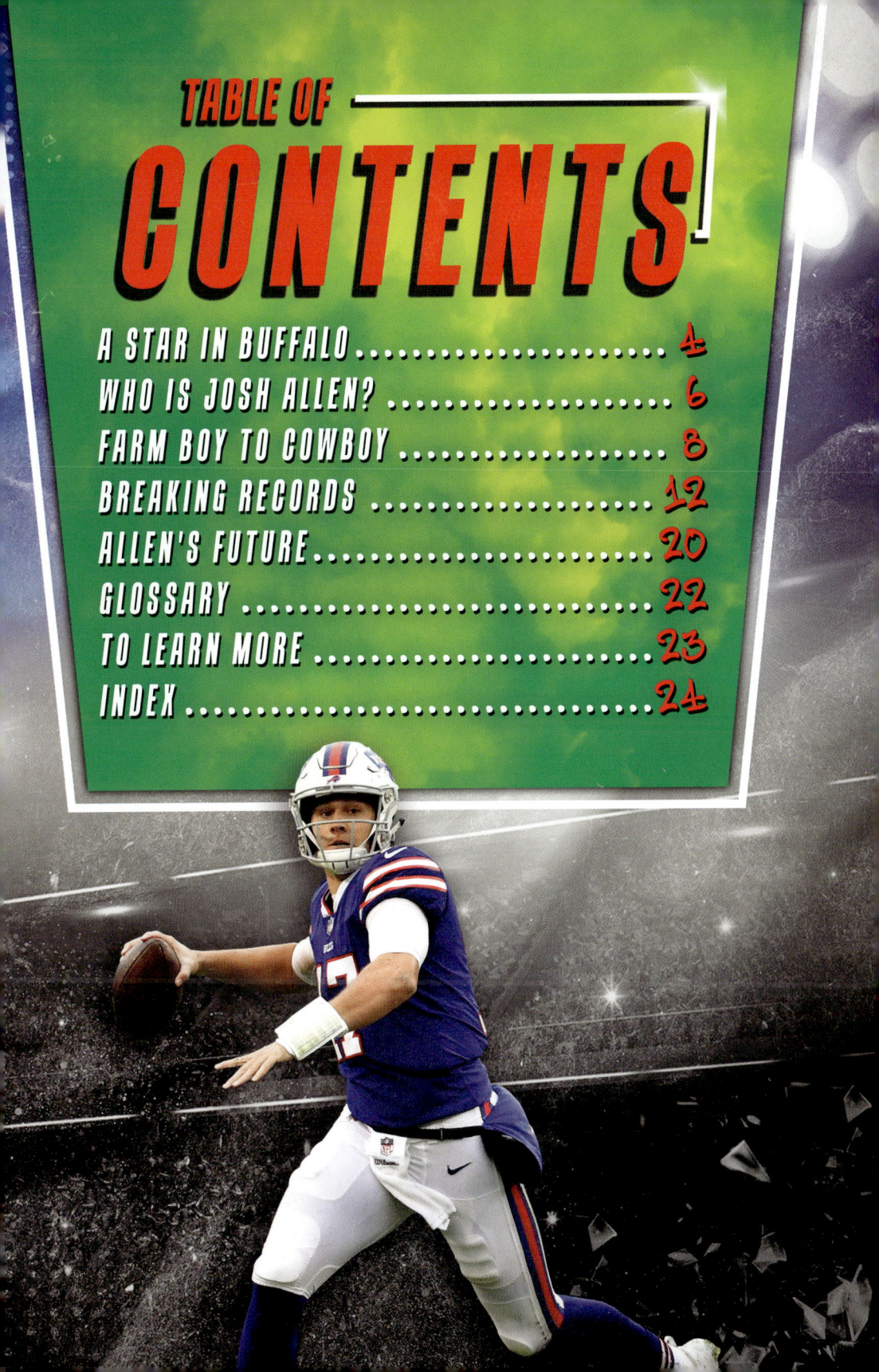

A STAR IN BUFFALO

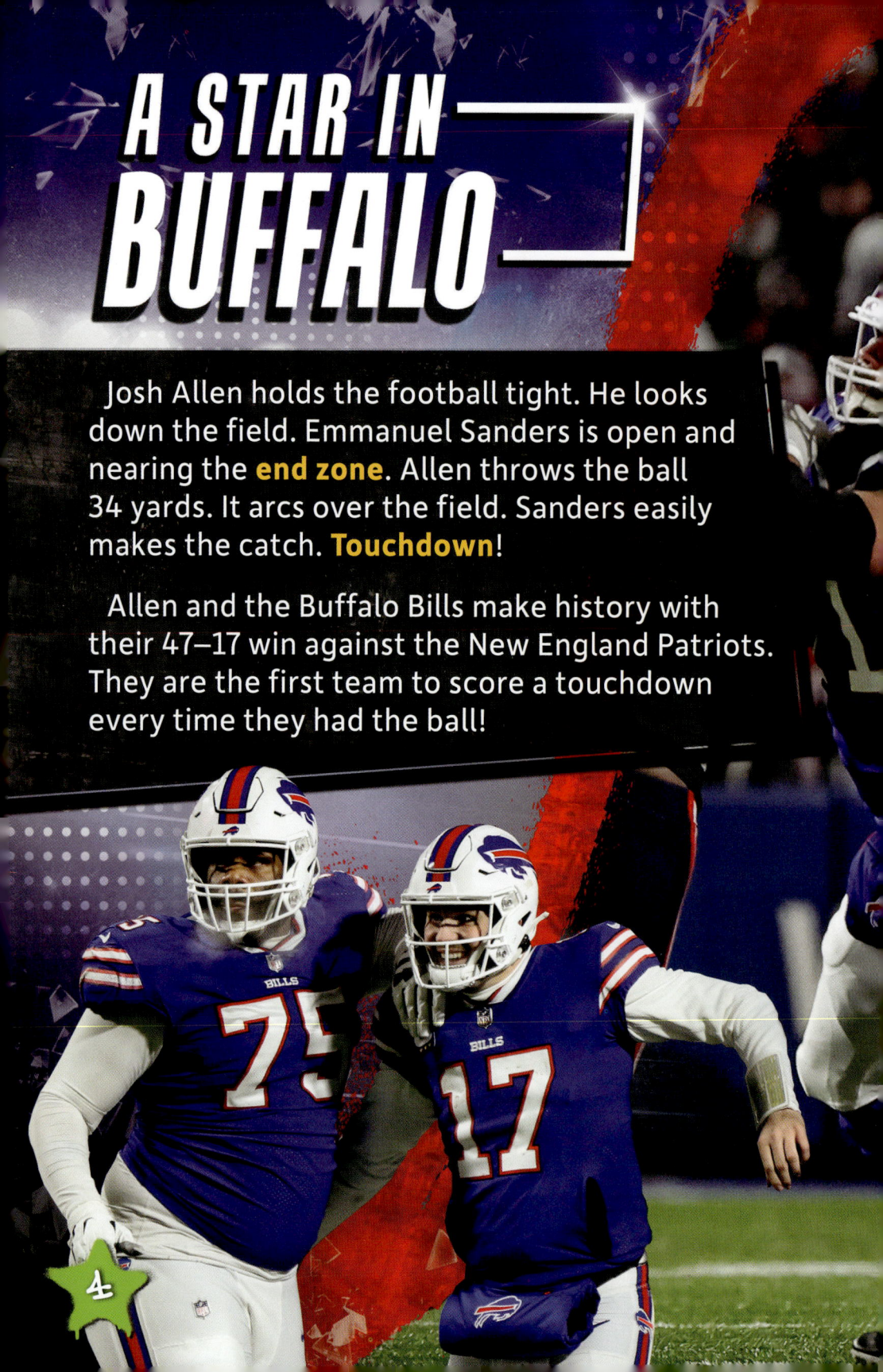

Josh Allen holds the football tight. He looks down the field. Emmanuel Sanders is open and nearing the **end zone**. Allen throws the ball 34 yards. It arcs over the field. Sanders easily makes the catch. **Touchdown**!

Allen and the Buffalo Bills make history with their 47–17 win against the New England Patriots. They are the first team to score a touchdown every time they had the ball!

WHO IS JOSH ALLEN?

Josh Allen is a record-breaking player in the **National Football League** (NFL). He is the **quarterback** for the Buffalo Bills. He is also one of the team captains. In his third season, he led the Bills to win their **division**. It was their first since 1995.

JOSH ALLEN

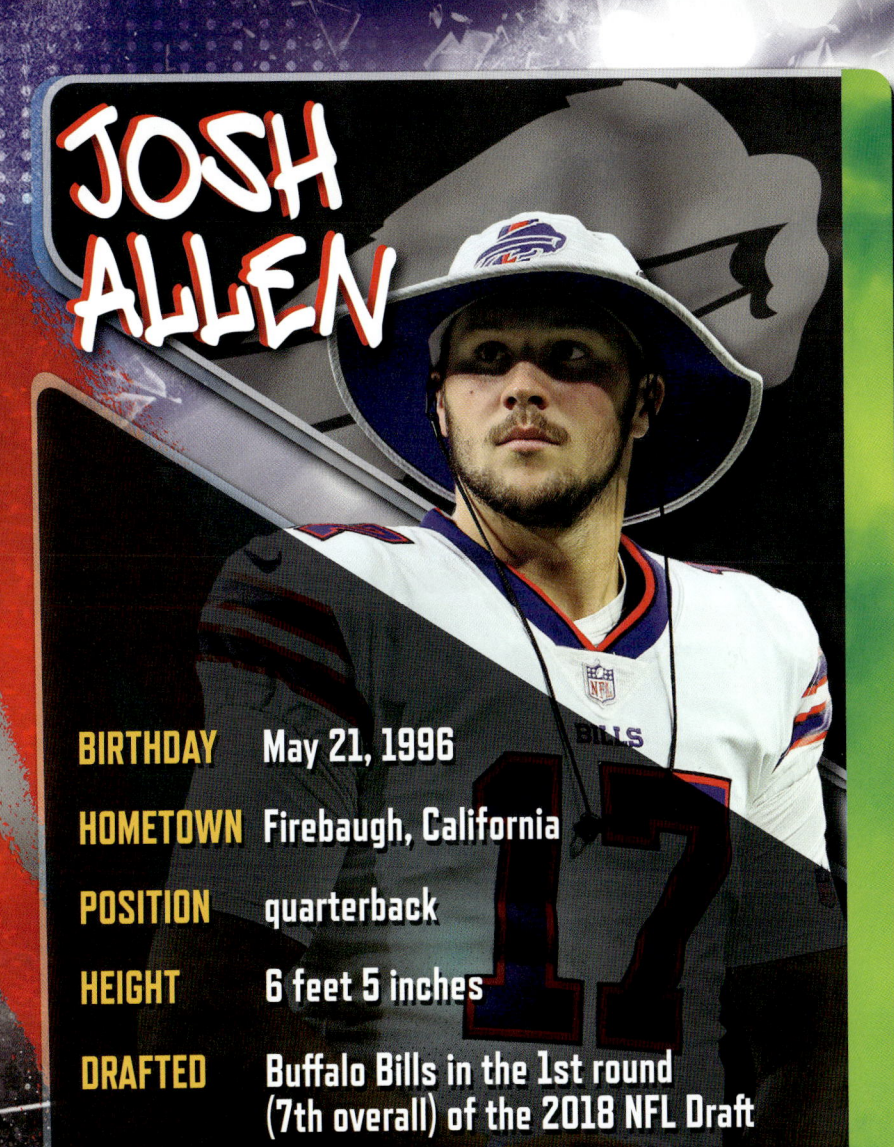

BIRTHDAY May 21, 1996

HOMETOWN Firebaugh, California

POSITION quarterback

HEIGHT 6 feet 5 inches

DRAFTED Buffalo Bills in the 1st round (7th overall) of the 2018 NFL Draft

PREGAME PLAYLIST

Allen enjoys listening to music before each game. Some of his favorite artists are Frank Sinatra, Elvis Presley, and Billy Joel.

FARM BOY TO COWBOY

Allen was born on May 21, 1996, in Firebaugh, California. He and his three siblings grew up on a farm. Allen helped with the crops and learned to value hard work.

The Allen family also loved sports. Allen's farm had a batting cage, basketball court, and volleyball court!

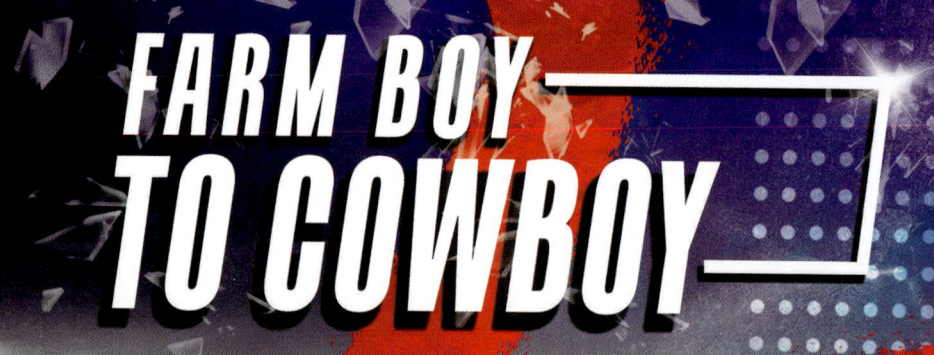

THAT'S NUTS!

ALLEN AND HIS FAMILY CONTINUE TO WORK ON THE FARM. THEY PLANTED PISTACHIO TREES IN 2021 AND PLAN TO HAVE 1,000 ACRES (405 HECTARES) OF PISTACHIOS!

ALLEN WITH HIS PARENTS IN 2018

9

Allen played many sports in high school. He showed a real talent for football.

But few colleges were interested in Allen. He was accepted at Reedley College and joined their football team. Then, a **scout** from the University of Wyoming saw him play. He joined the University of Wyoming Cowboys in 2015.

FAVORITES

FOOD

spicy
chicken wings

TV SHOW

The Office

OTHER SPORT

Formula One

HOBBY

golf

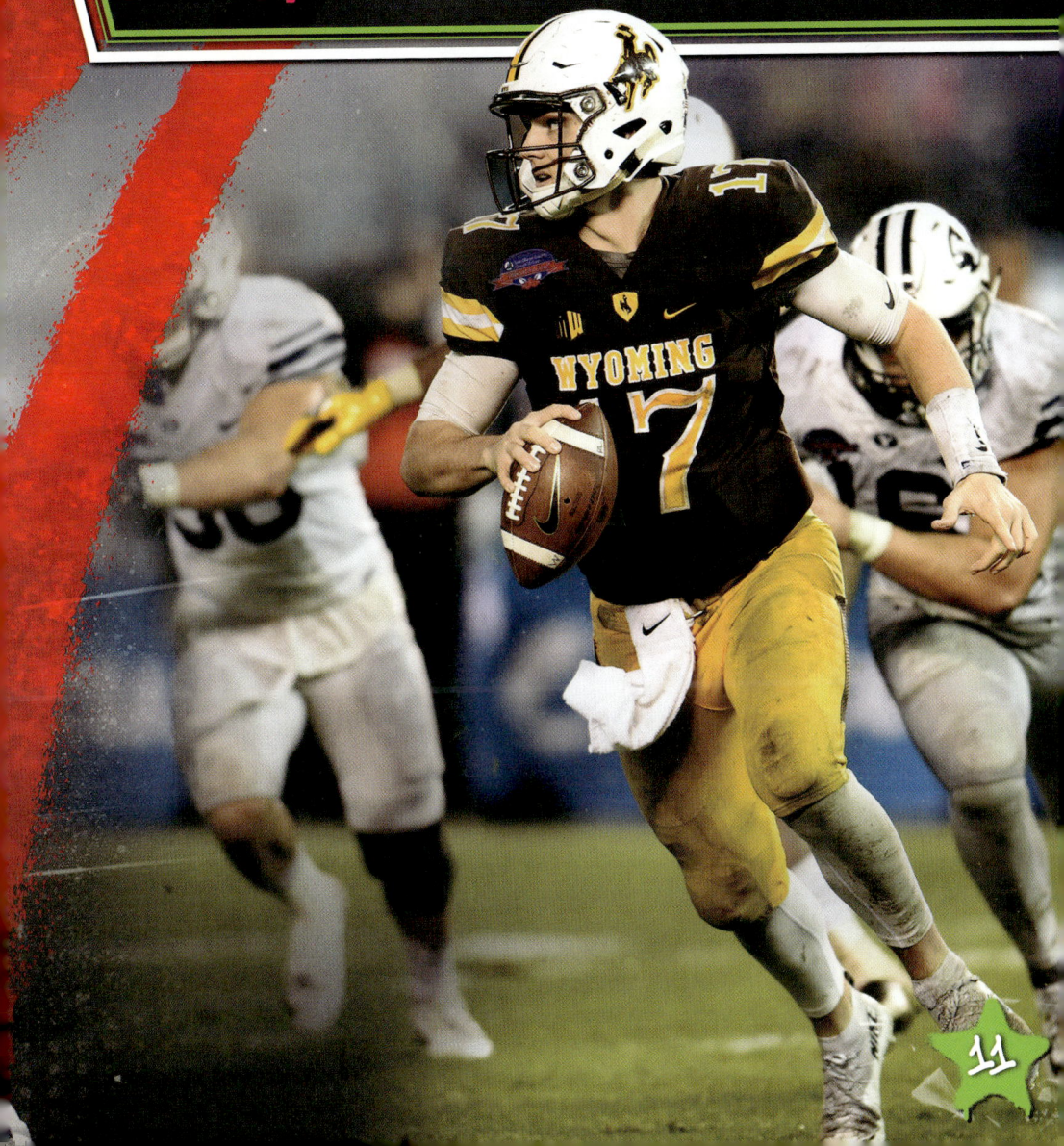

11

BREAKING RECORDS

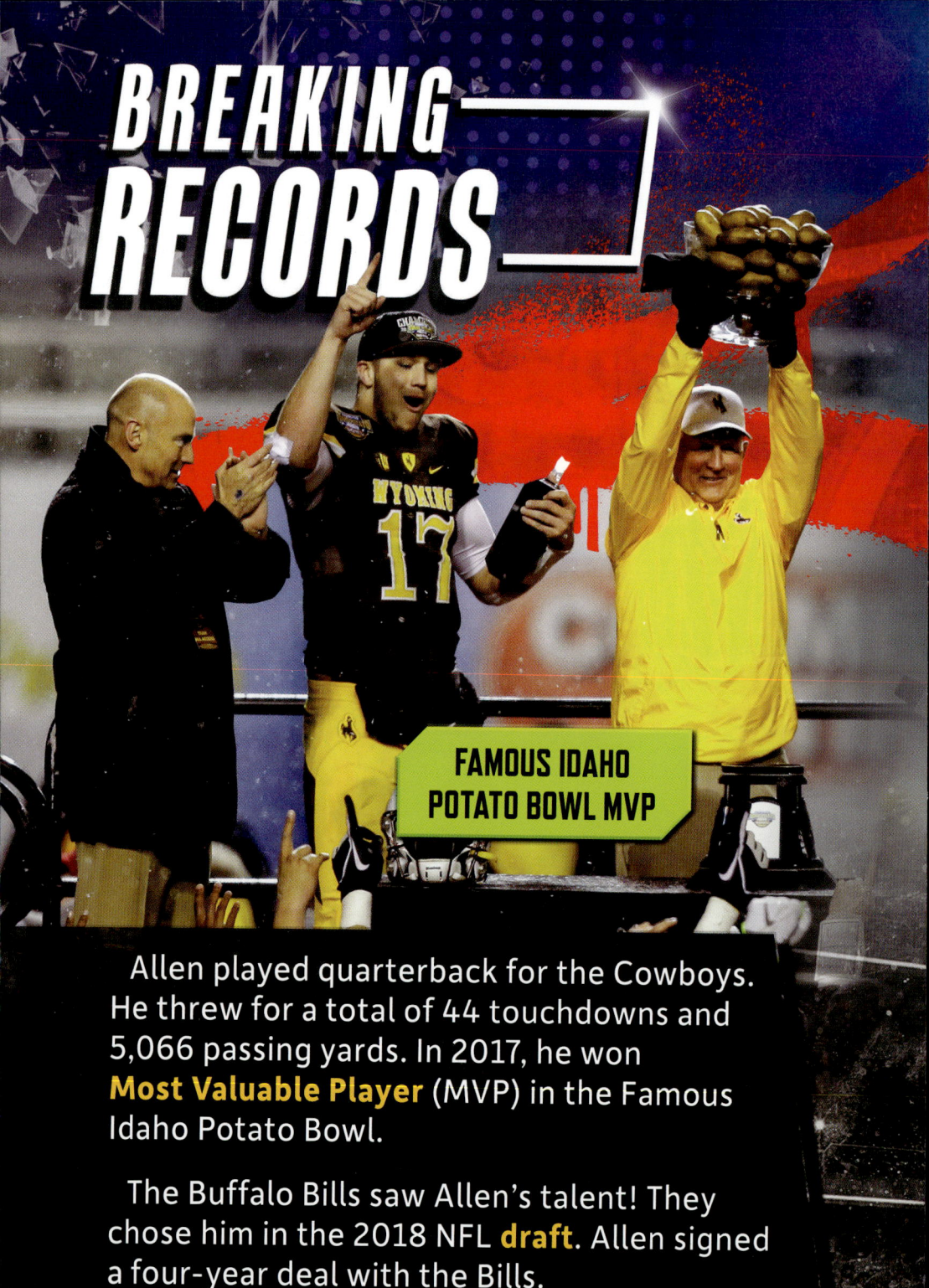

FAMOUS IDAHO POTATO BOWL MVP

Allen played quarterback for the Cowboys. He threw for a total of 44 touchdowns and 5,066 passing yards. In 2017, he won **Most Valuable Player** (MVP) in the Famous Idaho Potato Bowl.

The Buffalo Bills saw Allen's talent! They chose him in the 2018 NFL **draft**. Allen signed a four-year deal with the Bills.

JOSH ALLEN MAP

◉ **Buffalo Bills, Orchard Park, New York**

2018 to present

2018 NFL DRAFT

13

In 2018, Allen became the first quarterback in modern NFL history to run for at least 95 yards in three back-to-back games. He later helped the Bills make the 2019 **playoffs**.

14

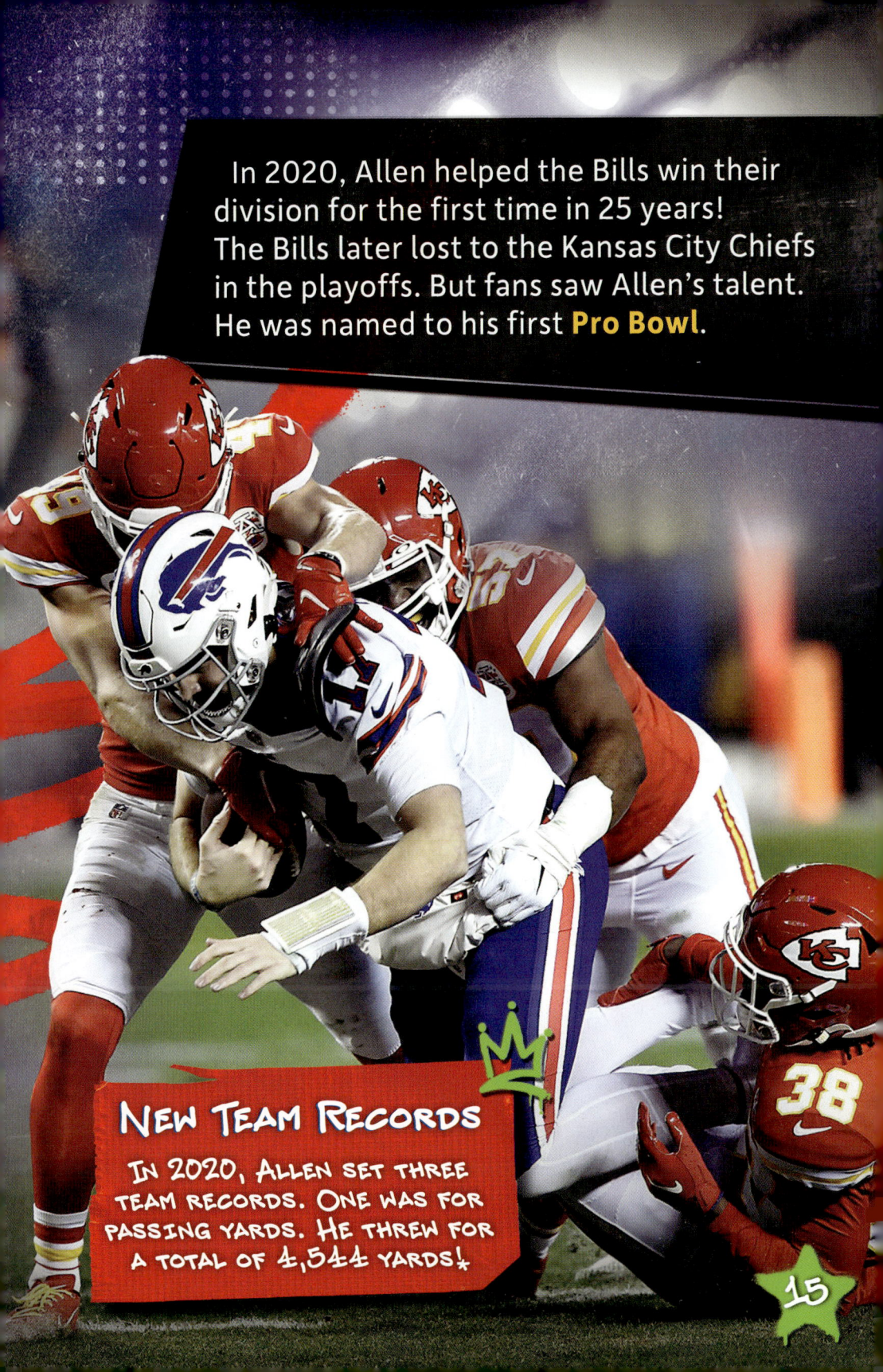

In 2020, Allen helped the Bills win their division for the first time in 25 years! The Bills later lost to the Kansas City Chiefs in the playoffs. But fans saw Allen's talent. He was named to his first **Pro Bowl**.

New Team Records

In 2020, Allen set three team records. One was for passing yards. He threw for a total of 4,544 yards!*

15

Allen helped the Bills win their division again in 2021. The team set an NFL record in the playoffs against the New England Patriots. Allen helped the team score every time they controlled the ball.

But the Bills lost their next game against the Chiefs.

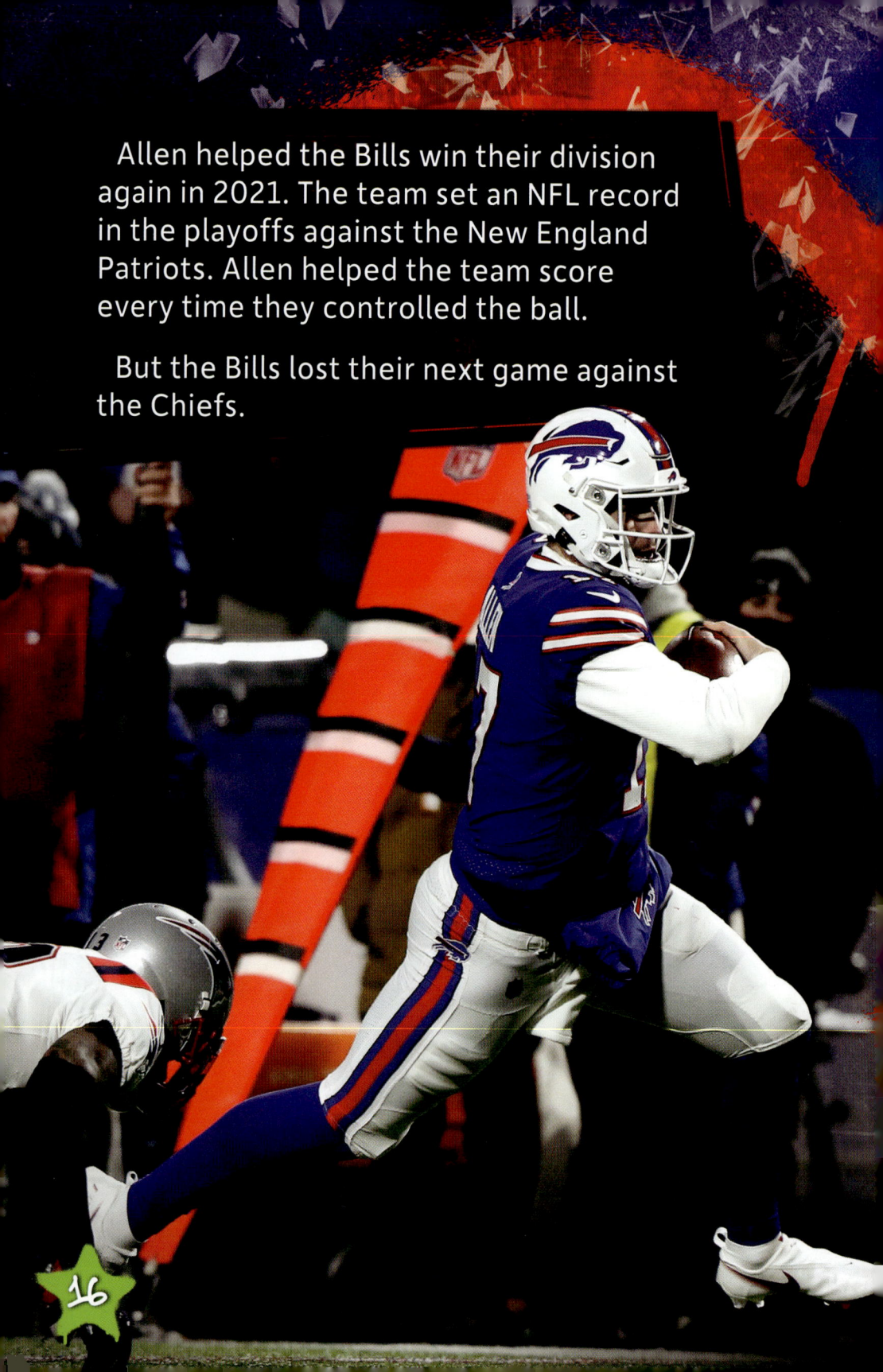

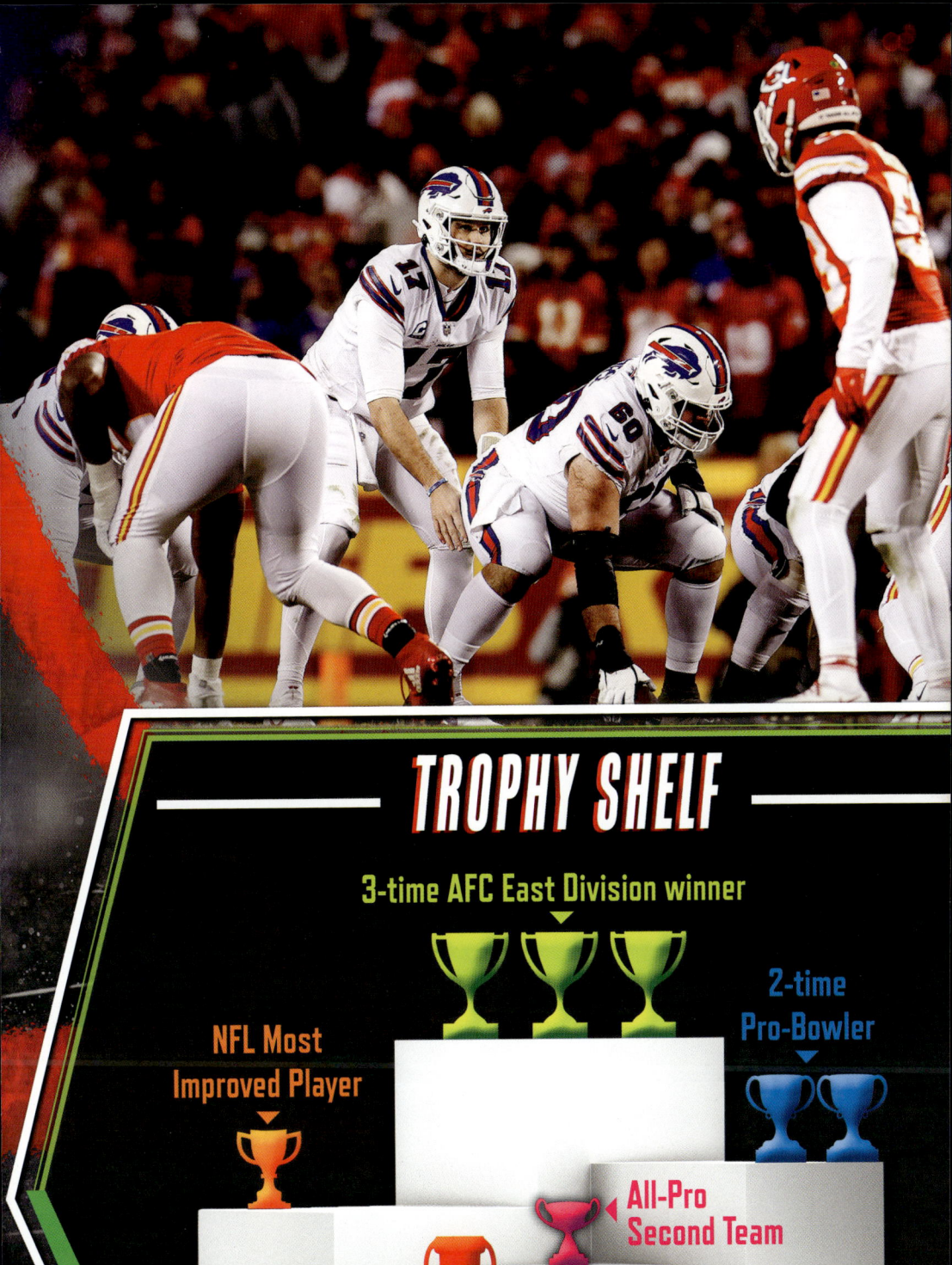

TROPHY SHELF

3-time AFC East Division winner

2-time Pro-Bowler

NFL Most Improved Player

All-Pro Second Team

Famous Idaho Potato Bowl MVP

17

In 2021, Allen signed to play with the Bills for another six years.

In 2022, Allen played against three former MVP quarterbacks. He beat them all! Allen led the Bills to another division win. He was also named to his second Pro Bowl. But the Bills' season ended with a playoff loss against the Cincinnati Bengals.

TIMELINE

— 2018 —
Allen is drafted by the Bills

— 2015 —
Allen joins the Cowboys

18

— 2020 —
Allen leads the Bills to win their division

— 2021 —
Allen signs a deal to play with the Bills for another six years

— 2022 —
Allen is named to the Pro Bowl for the second time

ALLEN'S FUTURE

Allen is giving back to people in his home and college states. In 2022, he worked with a company to give $10 million to people in need in Wyoming and California.

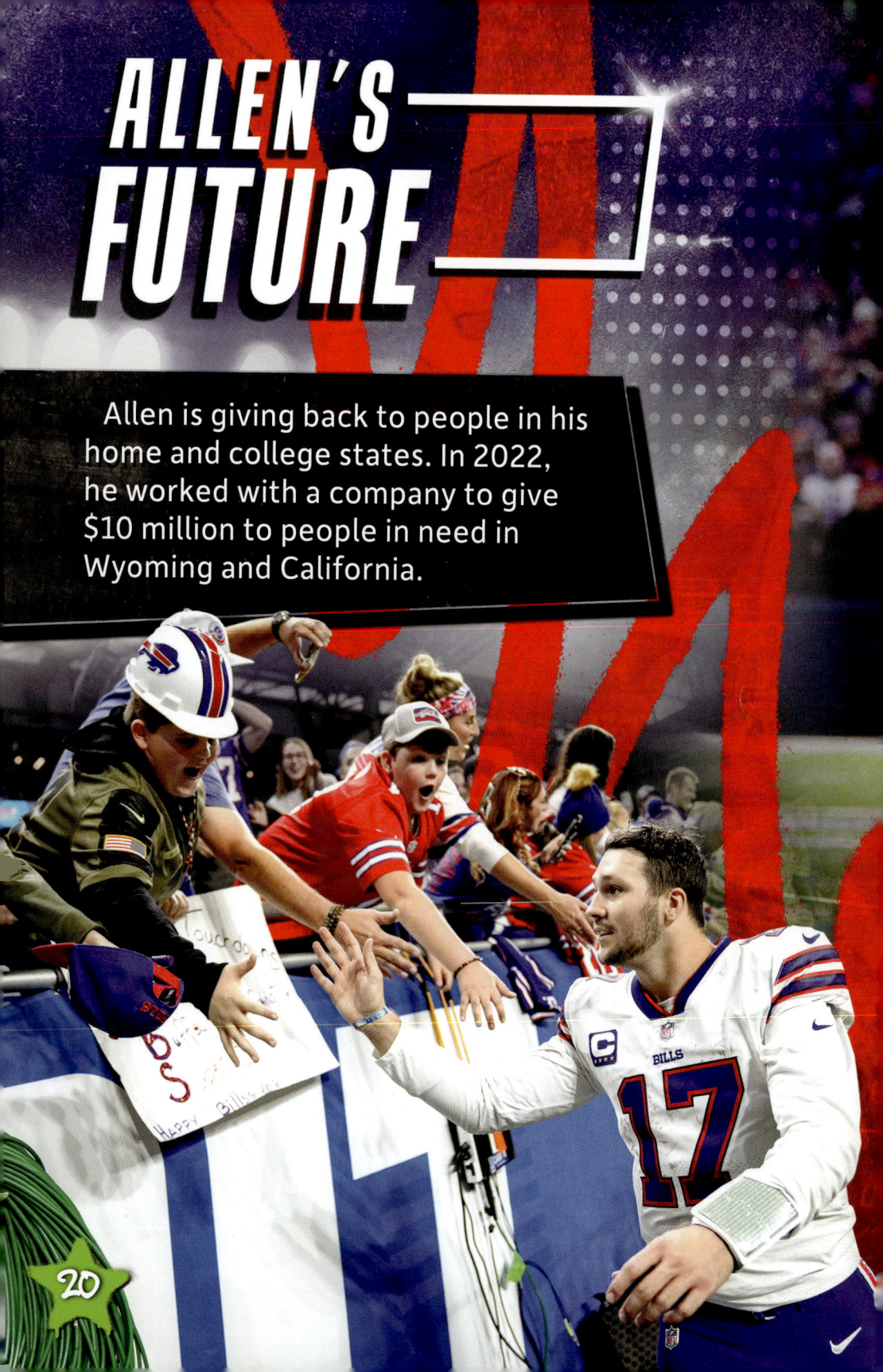

WHAT A RUSH!

In 2022, Allen became the first quarterback to throw for 4,000 yards and run for 750 yards in a season.

Today, Allen is on track to set more touchdown records. He is one of the best quarterbacks in the NFL. Allen dreams he and the Bills will win the **Super Bowl** soon!

GLOSSARY

division—a group of NFL teams from the same area that play against each other; there are eight divisions in the NFL.

draft—a process during which professional teams choose high school and college players to play for them

end zone—a part of a football field at each end; teams score points when they go into the end zone.

most valuable player—the best player in a year, game, or series; the most valuable player is often called the MVP.

National Football League—a professional football league in the United States; the National Football League is often called the NFL.

playoffs—games played after the regular season is over; playoff games determine which teams play in the championship game.

Pro Bowl—a game between the best players in the NFL

quarterback—a player on offense whose main job is to throw and hand off the ball

scout—a person who watches players in action and recommends them for a team

Super Bowl—the annual championship game of the National Football League

touchdown—a score that occurs when a team crosses into their opponent's end zone with the football; a touchdown is worth six points.

TO LEARN MORE

AT THE LIBRARY

Adamson, Thomas K. *Joe Burrow*. Minneapolis, Minn.: Bellwether Media, 2023.

Lowe, Alexander. *Josh Allen*. Minneapolis, Minn.: Lerner Publications, 2022.

Morey, Allan. *Dak Prescott*. Minneapolis, Minn.: Bellwether Media, 2023.

ON THE WEB

FACTSURFER

Factsurfer.com gives you a safe, fun way to find more information.

1. Go to www.factsurfer.com

2. Enter "Josh Allen" into the search box and click 🔍.

3. Select your book cover to see a list of related content.

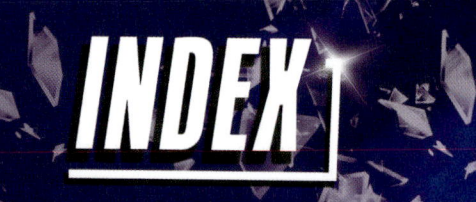

INDEX